Therapy Notes

A THERAPY NOTEBOOK WITH SECTIONS TO: COMPLETE BEFORE YOU HAVE THERAPY, TO RECORD OF YOUR MOOD, TO NOTE HOW YOUR THOUGHTS AFFECT THE WAY YOU FEEL, TO WRITE YOUR REFLECTIONS AFTER SESSIONS, TO RECORD PAINFUL MEMORIES, TO RECORD CRITICAL INCIDENTS IN YOUR LIFE, AND TO KEEP A RECORD OF YOUR DREAMS

Dr James Manning & Dr Nicola Ridgeway

Published by the West Suffolk CBT Service Ltd

Therapy notes

About the authors

Dr Nicola Ridgeway is a Consultant Clinical Psychologist and an accredited cognitive and behavioural therapist. She lectured on cognitive behaviour therapy (CBT) at the University of East Anglia, Norfolk, England, and the University of Essex for many years before becoming the Clinical Director of the West Suffolk CBT Service Ltd. Together with Dr James Manning she has co-authored several books on CBT.

Dr James Manning is a Consultant Clinical Psychologist and the Managing Director of the West Suffolk CBT Service. James has post-graduate qualifications in both Clinical Psychology and Counselling Psychology. He has regularly offered workshops and training to clinicians throughout the United Kingdom and continues to work as a therapist.

By the authors

Think About Your Thinking to Stop Depression

How to Help Your Loved One Overcome Depression

The Little Book on CBT for Depression

CBT Worksheets

CBT: What it is and how it works (2nd Edition)

My CBT Journal

CBT Worksheets for Anxiety

CBT Worksheets for Teenage Social Anxiety

Breaking free from social anxiety

Fused: A memoir of childhood OCD and adult obsession

How to befriend, tame, manage and teach your black dog called depression using CBT

How to use this notebook

This journal is designed for people who are having therapy or counselling sessions. You will get a lot more out of your therapy if you a) think about what you what you want to achieve before you have your therapy meetings and b) reflect on your therapy sessions after your meetings.

This journal has seven sections

- Section 1 -To complete before you have therapy

- Section 2 -To keep a record of your mood

- Section 3 - To note how your thoughts affect the way you feel

- Section 4 - To write your reflections after sessions.

- Section 5 - To record painful memories

- Section 6 - To record critical incidents in your life

- Section 7 - To keep a record of your dreams

If you run out of sheets and would like to print out a PDF of this book please email us at stoppingdepression@gmail.com telling us where you bought this book and we will send you a PDF file by return.

Problem list

A problem list can be very useful to create before having therapy or counselling. A problem list can help you to narrow your focus so that when you complete therapy you will be using your time and targeting your resources effectively. It will also help your therapist to focus his or her attention to help you make better use of your therapy time. Many of us are very good at identifying what doesn't feel right in our lives, and being as specific as possible about what your problems are will be very useful when completing therapy or counselling.

You may have decided to have therapy because you are feeling emotionally distressed, and it is quite common to experience problems with anxiety, worry, panic attacks, depression and anger. Feelings, however, are not the cause of your problem; they are a symptom of your problem. When you complete your problem list, it will be useful to think about what factors in your life are triggering your distressing emotions. Examples of problems could include:

- Difficulty asserting yourself in your relationships.

- Having low self-esteem.

- Difficulties managing workload.

- Neglecting yourself through the use of certain behaviours, drugs, food or alcohol.

- Avoiding activities, behaviours or certain types of interactions.

- Experiencing difficulties in how you react to your thoughts and feelings.

- Difficulties dealing with confrontation.

- Difficulties interacting the way that you want to with others.

- Being emotionally disconnected from others and/or expressing your feelings.

- Carrying out unhelpful safety behaviours that stop desired progression in life.

- Being highly self-critical.

- Feeling hijacked by your emotions.

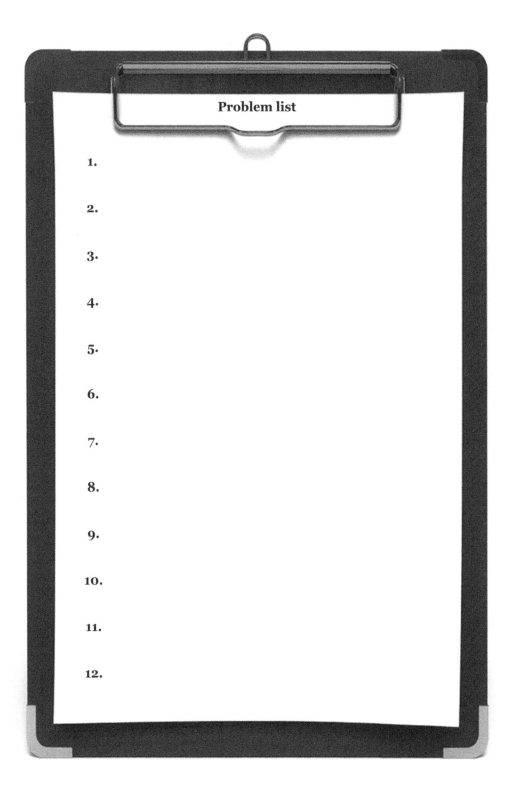

Problem list

1.

2.

3.

4.

5.

6.

7.

8.

9.

10.

11.

12.

Therapy preparation sheets

A therapy preparation sheet will help you to focus your mind on the problem that you are working on. Acknowledging that you have a problem is the first step that you will need to make in creating change. Working through the details of a problem can be very useful, as it can bring to mind the small things that tend to keep your problem in place. Later on, these details will help you to resolve the problem. An example has been completed on the next page. It can be helpful to complete therapy preparation sheets for each problem on your therapy list. Several blank sheets have been included in this book.

Therapy preparation sheet

Describe the problem that I have been experiencing

I keep arguing with my partner in front of my children. The arguments are often over pointless little things and they make my children anxious and upset.

How long has this problem been around for?

This problem has been around for as long as I can remember. We both have a problem backing down.

What may have triggered this problem?

Being told that I have done something wrong is the main trigger, or being criticised.

How have I attempted to resolve my problem?

I try to keep the conversation short if I see an argument beginning, but my partner then starts to become anxious that I am being distant.

What are the main things that keep my problem in place?

Arguing back generally makes it worse. If I criticise my partner back it can end up in a war that seems to go on for days.

What will I need to do to resolve this problem?

Find a different way to reacting to my partner's comments. It takes two people to keep the argument going.

How would my life be different without this problem?

Life would be more peaceful and there would be less negative energy floating around the house. The children would feel more relaxed.

Therapy preparation sheet (1)

Describe the problem that I have been experiencing.

How long has the problem been around for?

What may have triggered this problem?

Therapy preparation sheet (2)

How have I attempted to resolve my problem?

What are the main things that keep my problem in place?

What will I need to do to resolve this problem?

How would my life be different without this problem?

Therapy preparation sheet (1)

Describe the problem that I have been experiencing.

How long has the problem been around for?

What may have triggered this problem?

Therapy preparation sheet (2)

How have I attempted to resolve my problem?

What are the main things that keep my problem in place?

What will I need to do to resolve this problem?

How would my life be different without this problem?

Therapy preparation sheet (1)

Describe the problem that I have been experiencing.

How long has the problem been around for?

What may have triggered this problem?

Therapy preparation sheet (2)

How have I attempted to resolve my problem?

What are the main things that keep my problem in place?

What will I need to do to resolve this problem?

How would my life be different without this problem?

Therapy preparation sheet (1)

Describe the problem that I have been experiencing.

How long has the problem been around for?

What may have triggered this problem?

Therapy preparation sheet (2)

How have I attempted to resolve my problem?

What are the main things that keep my problem in place?

What will I need to do to resolve this problem?

How would my life be different without this problem?

Therapy preparation sheet (1)

Describe the problem that I have been experiencing.

How long has the problem been around for?

What may have triggered this problem?

Therapy preparation sheet (2)

How have I attempted to resolve my problem?

What are the main things that keep my problem in place?

What will I need to do to resolve this problem?

How would my life be different without this problem?

Therapy preparation sheet (1)

Describe the problem that I have been experiencing.

How long has the problem been around for?

What may have triggered this problem?

Therapy preparation sheet (2)

How have I attempted to resolve my problem?

What are the main things that keep my problem in place?

What will I need to do to resolve this problem?

How would my life be different without this problem?

Thought, feeling, physiology and behaviour diaries

Once a problem has been identified the completion of thought, feeling, physiology and behaviour diaries can be extremely useful. Generally, most of us live our lives automatically, without giving much thought to a) thinking about our thinking, b) how we react to our feelings or c) what makes us behave in the way that we do.

Completing a diary brings more of our automatic processes into awareness. Once these patterns are brought into our conscious awareness, we immediately have more choice about how to react. This is due to the fact that writing down information about the self encourages a process of stepping back and observing. This type of focussed detachment will automatically encourage the use of self-reflection. As soon as we start to consider what makes us think, feel or behave the way that we do, we engage the front part of the brain, which can often disengage when we become distressed.

In this section we have included two types of blank sheets for you to complete. A completed example is shown on the next page.

Thoughts, feelings & behaviour diary

Time: Date: Trigger situation	Thoughts, e.g., 'They must think that I'm an idiot'	Emotion, e.g., anxiety, anger, shame, disgust	Behaviour, e.g., avoid situation
12.00pm 6 June Disagreement with an opposing football coach.	'He's going along with the referee's decision because it's easier for him. My reaction shows that there is something wrong with me. He's laughing at me and thinks I'm an idiot.'	Anxiety, anger, guilt, shame.	Raise a formal protest. Think of some different ways in which I can get him back. Churn the situation over in my mind for a couple of days. Feel guilty and ashamed about the way that I am thinking.

Thoughts, feelings & behaviour diary

Time: Date: Trigger situation	Thoughts, e.g., 'They must think that I'm an idiot'	Emotion, e.g., anxiety, anger, shame, disgust	Behaviour, e.g., avoid situation

Thoughts, feelings & behaviour diary

Time: Date: Trigger situation	Thoughts, e.g., 'They must think that I'm an idiot'	Emotion, e.g., anxiety, anger, shame, disgust	Behaviour, e.g., avoid situation

Thoughts, feelings & behaviour diary

Time: Date: Trigger situation	Thoughts, e.g., 'They must think that I'm an idiot'	Emotion, e.g., anxiety, anger, shame, disgust	Behaviour, e.g., avoid situation

Thoughts, feelings & behaviour diary

Time: Date: Trigger situation	Thoughts, e.g., 'They must think that I'm an idiot'	Emotion, e.g., anxiety, anger, shame, disgust	Behaviour, e.g., avoid situation

Thoughts, feelings & behaviour diary

Time: Date: Trigger situation	Thoughts, e.g., 'They must think that I'm an idiot'	Emotion, e.g., anxiety, anger, shame, disgust	Behaviour, e.g., avoid situation

Thoughts, feelings & behaviour diary

Time: Date: Trigger situation	Thoughts, e.g., 'They must think that I'm an idiot'	Emotion, e.g., anxiety, anger, shame, disgust	Behaviour, e.g., avoid situation

Thought, emotion, physiology, and behaviour sheet

Day:

Time:

Trigger situation:

Thoughts:

Physiological reactions

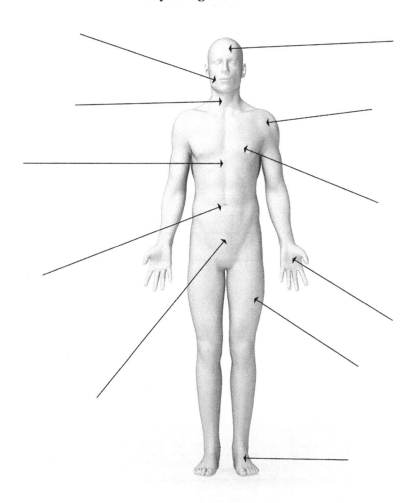

Emotion:

Behaviour:

Thought, emotion, physiology, and behaviour sheet

Day:

Time:

Trigger situation:

Thoughts:

Physiological reactions

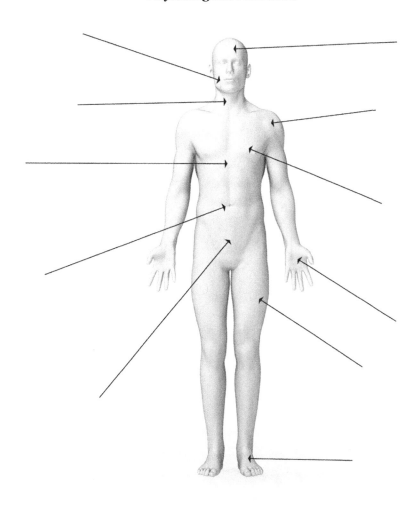

Emotion:

Behaviour:

Thought, emotion, physiology, and behaviour sheet

Day:

Time:

Trigger situation:

Thoughts:

Physiological reactions

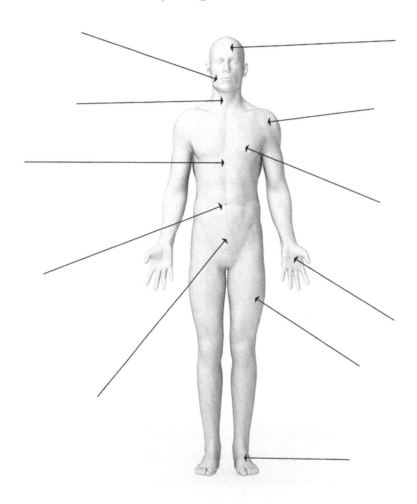

Emotion:

Behaviour:

Thought, emotion, physiology, and behaviour sheet

Day:

Time:

Trigger situation:

Thoughts:

Physiological reactions

Emotion:

Behaviour:

Thought, emotion, physiology, and behaviour sheet

Day:

Time:

Trigger situation:

Thoughts:

Physiological reactions

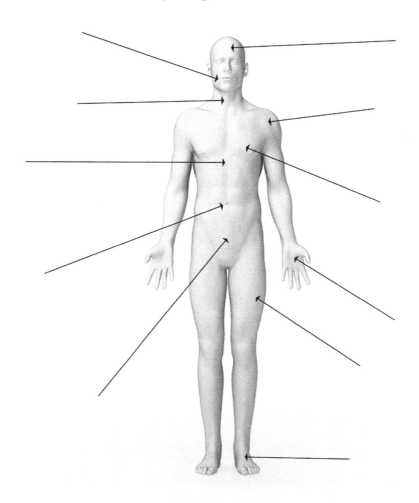

Emotion:

Behaviour:

Thought, emotion, physiology, and behaviour sheet

Day:

Time:

Trigger situation:

Thoughts:

Physiological reactions

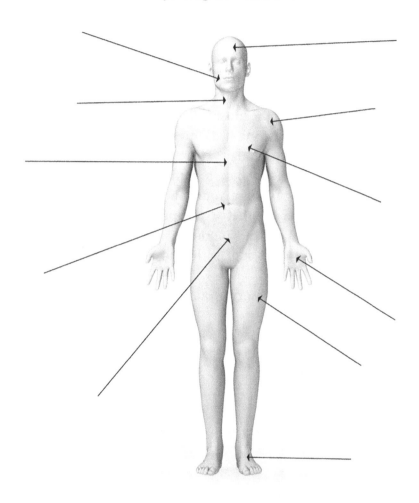

Emotion:

Behaviour:

Mood diaries

Mood diaries are very useful for keeping track of your mood and becoming aware of what types of activity result in mood changes. Most of the time memory alone is unreliable when it comes to recalling what activities impact on our mood. Often the most valid way to assess your mood is to make a record while you are experiencing it. Depression in particular can result in fluctuations in mood throughout the day. There may also be aspects of your life or behaviours that you engage in that have a significant impact on your mood that you are not aware of. Keeping track of your mood will help you to identify external or internal aspects of your life that are keeping your emotional distress in place. If you notice fluctuations in your mood this is also a potential area for discussion with your counsellor, therapist or with your psychiatrist/GP if you are receiving medication.

We have included tables for you to observe your mood in this section.

Mood Diary

Please use this diary to keep a record of your mood. For each time period give yourself a score between 0 and 10 where 10 is the most that you can experience a feeling.

For the positive feeling box please rate how positive you felt during each time period as a whole. Examples of positivity may include being interested, excited, enthusiastic, strong, proud etc.

For the negative feeling box please rate how negative you felt during the time period. Examples of negativity may include feeling distressed, hostile, afraid, upset, ashamed and such like.

Day _____ Date _____

Time period	Positive feeling 0 to 10	Negative feeling 0 to 10
6am to 12pm		
12pm to 6pm		
6pm to 12am		

Day _____ Date _____

Time period	Positive feeling 0 to 10	Negative feeling 0 to 10
6am to 12pm		
12pm to 6pm		
6pm to 12am		

Day _____ Date _____

Time period	Positive feeling 0 to 10	Negative feeling 0 to 10
6am to 12pm		
12pm to 6pm		
6pm to 12am		

Day _____ Date _____

Time period	Positive feeling 0 to 10	Negative feeling 0 to 10
6am to 12pm		
12pm to 6pm		
6pm to 12am		

Day _____ Date _____

Time period	Positive feeling 0 to 10	Negative feeling 0 to 10
6am to 12pm		
12pm to 6pm		
6pm to 12am		

Day _____ Date _____

Time period	Positive feeling 0 to 10	Negative feeling 0 to 10
6am to 12pm		
12pm to 6pm		
6pm to 12am		

Day _____ Date _____

Time period	Positive feeling 0 to 10	Negative feeling 0 to 10
6am to 12pm		
12pm to 6pm		
6pm to 12am		

Day _____ Date _____

Time period	Positive feeling 0 to 10	Negative feeling 0 to 10
6am to 12pm		
12pm to 6pm		
6pm to 12am		

Day _____ Date _____

Time period	Positive feeling 0 to 10	Negative feeling 0 to 10
6am to 12pm		
12pm to 6pm		
6pm to 12am		

Mood Diary

Please use this diary to keep a record of your mood. For each time period give yourself a score between 0 and 10 where 10 is the most that you can experience a feeling.

For the positive feeling box please rate how positive you felt during each time period as a whole. Examples of positivity may include being interested, excited, enthusiastic, strong, proud etc.

For the negative feeling box please rate how negative you felt during the time period. Examples of negativity may include feeling distressed, hostile, afraid, upset, ashamed and such like.

Day **Date**

Time period	Positive feeling 0 to 10	Negative feeling 0 to 10
6am to 12pm		
12pm to 6pm		
6pm to 12am		

Day **Date**

Time period	Positive feeling 0 to 10	Negative feeling 0 to 10
6am to 12pm		
12pm to 6pm		
6pm to 12am		

Day **Date**

Time period	Positive feeling 0 to 10	Negative feeling 0 to 10
6am to 12pm		
12pm to 6pm		
6pm to 12am		

Day **Date**

Time period	Positive feeling 0 to 10	Negative feeling 0 to 10
6am to 12pm		
12pm to 6pm		
6pm to 12am		

Day **Date**

Time period	Positive feeling 0 to 10	Negative feeling 0 to 10
6am to 12pm		
12pm to 6pm		
6pm to 12am		

Day **Date**

Time period	Positive feeling 0 to 10	Negative feeling 0 to 10
6am to 12pm		
12pm to 6pm		
6pm to 12am		

Day **Date**

Time period	Positive feeling 0 to 10	Negative feeling 0 to 10
6am to 12pm		
12pm to 6pm		
6pm to 12am		

Day **Date**

Time period	Positive feeling 0 to 10	Negative feeling 0 to 10
6am to 12pm		
12pm to 6pm		
6pm to 12am		

Mood Diary

Please use this diary to keep a record of your mood. For each time period give yourself a score between 0 and 10 where 10 is the most that you can experience a feeling.

For the positive feeling box please rate how positive you felt during each time period as a whole. Examples of positivity may include being interested, excited, enthusiastic, strong, proud etc.

For the negative feeling box please rate how negative you felt during the time period. Examples of negativity may include feeling distressed, hostile, afraid, upset, ashamed and such like.

Day   **Date**

Time period	Positive feeling 0 to 10	Negative feeling 0 to 10
6am to 12pm		
12pm to 6pm		
6pm to 12am		

Day   **Date**

Time period	Positive feeling 0 to 10	Negative feeling 0 to 10
6am to 12pm		
12pm to 6pm		
6pm to 12am		

Day   **Date**

Time period	Positive feeling 0 to 10	Negative feeling 0 to 10
6am to 12pm		
12pm to 6pm		
6pm to 12am		

Day   **Date**

Time period	Positive feeling 0 to 10	Negative feeling 0 to 10
6am to 12pm		
12pm to 6pm		
6pm to 12am		

Day   **Date**

Time period	Positive feeling 0 to 10	Negative feeling 0 to 10
6am to 12pm		
12pm to 6pm		
6pm to 12am		

Day   **Date**

Time period	Positive feeling 0 to 10	Negative feeling 0 to 10
6am to 12pm		
12pm to 6pm		
6pm to 12am		

Day   **Date**

Time period	Positive feeling 0 to 10	Negative feeling 0 to 10
6am to 12pm		
12pm to 6pm		
6pm to 12am		

Day   **Date**

Time period	Positive feeling 0 to 10	Negative feeling 0 to 10
6am to 12pm		
12pm to 6pm		
6pm to 12am		

Day   **Date**

Time period	Positive feeling 0 to 10	Negative feeling 0 to 10
6am to 12pm		
12pm to 6pm		
6pm to 12am		

Mood Diary

Please use this diary to keep a record of your mood. For each time period give yourself a score between 0 and 10 where 10 is the most that you can experience a feeling.

For the positive feeling box please rate how positive you felt during each time period as a whole. Examples of positivity may include being interested, excited, enthusiastic, strong, proud etc.

For the negative feeling box please rate how negative you felt during the time period. Examples of negativity may include feeling distressed, hostile, afraid, upset, ashamed and such like.

Day

Time period	Positive feeling 0 to 10	Negative feeling 0 to 10
6am to 12pm		
12pm to 6pm		
6pm to 12am		

Date

Day

Time period	Positive feeling 0 to 10	Negative feeling 0 to 10
6am to 12pm		
12pm to 6pm		
6pm to 12am		

Date

Day

Time period	Positive feeling 0 to 10	Negative feeling 0 to 10
6am to 12pm		
12pm to 6pm		
6pm to 12am		

Date

Day

Time period	Positive feeling 0 to 10	Negative feeling 0 to 10
6am to 12pm		
12pm to 6pm		
6pm to 12am		

Date

Day

Time period	Positive feeling 0 to 10	Negative feeling 0 to 10
6am to 12pm		
12pm to 6pm		
6pm to 12am		

Date

Day

Time period	Positive feeling 0 to 10	Negative feeling 0 to 10
6am to 12pm		
12pm to 6pm		
6pm to 12am		

Date

Day

Time period	Positive feeling 0 to 10	Negative feeling 0 to 10
6am to 12pm		
12pm to 6pm		
6pm to 12am		

Date

Day

Time period	Positive feeling 0 to 10	Negative feeling 0 to 10
6am to 12pm		
12pm to 6pm		
6pm to 12am		

Date

Day

Time period	Positive feeling 0 to 10	Negative feeling 0 to 10
6am to 12pm		
12pm to 6pm		
6pm to 12am		

Date

Mood Diary

Please use this diary to keep a record of your mood. For each time period give yourself a score between 0 and 10 where 10 is the most that you can experience a feeling.

For the positive feeling box please rate how positive you felt during each time period as a whole. Examples of positivity may include being interested, excited, enthusiastic, strong, proud etc.

For the negative feeling box please rate how negative you felt during the time period. Examples of negativity may include feeling distressed, hostile, afraid, upset, ashamed and such like.

Day ____   Date ____

Time period	Positive feeling 0 to 10	Negative feeling 0 to 10
6am to 12pm		
12pm to 6pm		
6pm to 12am		

Day ____   Date ____

Time period	Positive feeling 0 to 10	Negative feeling 0 to 10
6am to 12pm		
12pm to 6pm		
6pm to 12am		

Day ____   Date ____

Time period	Positive feeling 0 to 10	Negative feeling 0 to 10
6am to 12pm		
12pm to 6pm		
6pm to 12am		

Day ____   Date ____

Time period	Positive feeling 0 to 10	Negative feeling 0 to 10
6am to 12pm		
12pm to 6pm		
6pm to 12am		

Day ____   Date ____

Time period	Positive feeling 0 to 10	Negative feeling 0 to 10
6am to 12pm		
12pm to 6pm		
6pm to 12am		

Day ____   Date ____

Time period	Positive feeling 0 to 10	Negative feeling 0 to 10
6am to 12pm		
12pm to 6pm		
6pm to 12am		

Day ____   Date ____

Time period	Positive feeling 0 to 10	Negative feeling 0 to 10
6am to 12pm		
12pm to 6pm		
6pm to 12am		

Day ____   Date ____

Time period	Positive feeling 0 to 10	Negative feeling 0 to 10
6am to 12pm		
12pm to 6pm		
6pm to 12am		

Day ____   Date ____

Time period	Positive feeling 0 to 10	Negative feeling 0 to 10
6am to 12pm		
12pm to 6pm		
6pm to 12am		

Session notes

It is often helpful to write down your thoughts immediately after sessions while they are still fresh in your mind. So much information can be discussed in sessions that much of it can be quickly forgotten.

This section is for you to record details of your sessions. It will also serve as a handy memoir that you can look back over in the future when you have left your current problems behind.

Session 1 - Date_____

Session 2 - Date_____

Session 3 - Date_____

Session 4 - Date_____

Session 5 - Date_____

Session 6 - Date_____

Session 7 - Date_____

Session 8 - Date_____

Session 9 - Date_____

Session 10 - Date_____

Session 11 - Date_____

Session 12 - Date_____

Session 14 - Date_____

Session 15 - Date_____

Session 16 - Date_____

Session 17 - Date_____

Session 20 - Date_____

Session 23 - Date_____

Session 25 - Date_____

Session 26 - Date_____

Session 27 - Date_____

Session 29 - Date_____

Session 31 - Date_____

SECTION 5

Memories

Many people find that memories from the past can still affect the way that they feel. When this occurs it is highly likely that the memory has not been processed properly by the mind. Unprocessed memories can be triggered by reminders that occur outside of awareness, for example, particular people, places, smells, sounds or other information picked up by our senses. When unprocessed memories are triggered we can often start to feel emotionally distressed, but yet not really know why or have a sensible explanation for how we feel. If this occurs your therapist or counsellor may help you to find your unprocessed memories and help you to talk about them. This section has tables for you to record your distressing memories so that you can discuss them with your therapist, psychologist or counsellor.

Title of memory _____

How old were you when your memory occurred _____

How distressing is the memory (score between 0 and 10 whee 10 is the most distressing) _____

How vivid is the memory (score between 0 and 10 where 10 is the most distressing) _____

What negative thoughts go with this memory

_____

_____

Describe your memory in as much detail as possible below. Please include as much sensory information as possible, (for example, smells, what you saw, how you felt).

Title of memory _____

How old were you when your memory occurred _____

How distressing is the memory (score between 0 and 10 whee 10 is the most distressing) _____

How vivid is the memory (score between 0 and 10 where 10 is the most distressing) _____

What negative thoughts go with this memory

_____

_____

Describe your memory in as much detail as possible below. Please include as much sensory information as possible, (for example, smells, what you saw, how you felt).

Title of memory _____

How old were you when your memory occurred _____

How distressing is the memory (score between 0 and 10 whee 10 is the most distressing) _____

How vivid is the memory (score between 0 and 10 where 10 is the most distressing) _____

What negative thoughts go with this memory

_____

_____

Describe your memory in as much detail as possible below. Please include as much sensory information as possible, (for example, smells, what you saw, how you felt).

Title of memory _____

How old were you when your memory occurred _____

How distressing is the memory (score between 0 and 10 whee 10 is the most distressing) _____

How vivid is the memory (score between 0 and 10 where 10 is the most distressing) _____

What negative thoughts go with this memory

_____

_____

Describe your memory in as much detail as possible below. Please include as much sensory information as possible, (for example, smells, what you saw, how you felt).

Title of memory _____

How old were you when your memory occurred _____

How distressing is the memory (score between 0 and 10 whee 10 is the most distressing) _____

How vivid is the memory (score between 0 and 10 where 10 is the most distressing) _____

What negative thoughts go with this memory

_____

_____

Describe your memory in as much detail as possible below. Please include as much sensory information as possible, (for example, smells, what you saw, how you felt).

Title of memory _____

How old were you when your memory occurred _____

How distressing is the memory (score between 0 and 10 whee 10 is the most distressing) _____

How vivid is the memory (score between 0 and 10 where 10 is the most distressing) _____

What negative thoughts go with this memory

_____

_____

Describe your memory in as much detail as possible below. Please include as much sensory information as possible, (for example, smells, what you saw, how you felt).

Title of memory _____

How old were you when your memory occurred _____

How distressing is the memory (score between 0 and 10 whee 10 is the most distressing) _____

How vivid is the memory (score between 0 and 10 where 10 is the most distressing) _____

What negative thoughts go with this memory

_____

_____

Describe your memory in as much detail as possible below. Please include as much sensory information as possible, (for example, smells, what you saw, how you felt).

Title of memory _____

How old were you when your memory occurred _____

How distressing is the memory (score between 0 and 10 whee 10 is the most distressing) _____

How vivid is the memory (score between 0 and 10 where 10 is the most distressing) _____

What negative thoughts go with this memory

_____

_____

Describe your memory in as much detail as possible below. Please include as much sensory information as possible, (for example, smells, what you saw, how you felt).

Title of memory _____

How old were you when your memory occurred _____

How distressing is the memory (score between 0 and 10 whee 10 is the most distressing) _____

How vivid is the memory (score between 0 and 10 where 10 is the most distressing) _____

What negative thoughts go with this memory

_____

_____

Describe your memory in as much detail as possible below. Please include as much sensory information as possible, (for example, smells, what you saw, how you felt).

Title of memory _____

How old were you when your memory occurred _____

How distressing is the memory (score between 0 and 10 whee 10 is the most distressing) _____

How vivid is the memory (score between 0 and 10 where 10 is the most distressing) _____

What negative thoughts go with this memory

_____

_____

Describe your memory in as much detail as possible below. Please include as much sensory information as possible, (for example, smells, what you saw, how you felt).

Title of memory _____

How old were you when your memory occurred _____

How distressing is the memory (score between 0 and 10 whee 10 is the most distressing) _____

How vivid is the memory (score between 0 and 10 where 10 is the most distressing) _____

What negative thoughts go with this memory

_____

_____

Describe your memory in as much detail as possible below. Please include as much sensory information as possible, (for example, smells, what you saw, how you felt).

Title of memory _____

How old were you when your memory occurred _____

How distressing is the memory (score between 0 and 10 whee 10 is the most distressing) _____

How vivid is the memory (score between 0 and 10 where 10 is the most distressing) _____

What negative thoughts go with this memory

_____

_____

Describe your memory in as much detail as possible below. Please include as much sensory information as possible, (for example, smells, what you saw, how you felt).

Title of memory _____

How old were you when your memory occurred _____

How distressing is the memory (score between 0 and 10 whee 10 is the most distressing) _____

How vivid is the memory (score between 0 and 10 where 10 is the most distressing) _____

What negative thoughts go with this memory

_____

_____

Describe your memory in as much detail as possible below. Please include as much sensory information as possible, (for example, smells, what you saw, how you felt).

Title of memory _____

How old were you when your memory occurred _____

How distressing is the memory (score between 0 and 10 whee 10 is the most distressing) _____

How vivid is the memory (score between 0 and 10 where 10 is the most distressing) _____

What negative thoughts go with this memory

_____

_____

Describe your memory in as much detail as possible below. Please include as much sensory information as possible, (for example, smells, what you saw, how you felt).

Title of memory _____

How old were you when your memory occurred _____

How distressing is the memory (score between 0 and 10 whee 10 is the most distressing) _____

How vivid is the memory (score between 0 and 10 where 10 is the most distressing) _____

What negative thoughts go with this memory

_____

_____

Describe your memory in as much detail as possible below. Please include as much sensory information as possible, (for example, smells, what you saw, how you felt).

Title of memory _____

How old were you when your memory occurred _____

How distressing is the memory (score between 0 and 10 whee 10 is the most distressing) _____

How vivid is the memory (score between 0 and 10 where 10 is the most distressing) _____

What negative thoughts go with this memory

_____

_____

Describe your memory in as much detail as possible below. Please include as much sensory information as possible, (for example, smells, what you saw, how you felt).

Title of memory _____

How old were you when your memory occurred _____

How distressing is the memory (score between 0 and 10 whee 10 is the most distressing) _____

How vivid is the memory (score between 0 and 10 where 10 is the most distressing) _____

What negative thoughts go with this memory

_____

_____

Describe your memory in as much detail as possible below. Please include as much sensory information as possible, (for example, smells, what you saw, how you felt).

Critical incidents

Between therapy sessions life events may occur that distress us, we might be reminded about painful episodes from our pasts, or we may have negative thoughts or ideas. When such events occur it can often be very helpful to write down what happed for later discussion with your therapist or counsellor. Use this section to record situations that upset you or distress you.

Time date _____

Critical incident_____

How distressing was the incident (score between 0 and 10 whee 10 is the most distressing) _____

What negative thoughts go with this incident

_____

_____

_____

Describe the incident as much detail as possible below. Please include as much information as possible, (for example, how you felt, what happened, how you reacted).

Time date _____

Critical incident_____

How distressing was the incident (score between 0 and 10 whee 10 is the most distressing) _____

What negative thoughts go with this incident

_____

_____

_____

Describe the incident as much detail as possible below. Please include as much information as possible, (for example, how you felt, what happened, how you reacted).

Time date _____

Critical incident_____

How distressing was the incident (score between 0 and 10 whee 10 is the most distressing) _____

What negative thoughts go with this incident

_____

_____

_____

Describe the incident as much detail as possible below. Please include as much information as possible, (for example, how you felt, what happened, how you reacted).

Time date _____

Critical incident_____

How distressing was the incident (score between 0 and 10 whee 10 is the most distressing) _____

What negative thoughts go with this incident

_____

_____

_____

Describe the incident as much detail as possible below. Please include as much information as possible, (for example, how you felt, what happened, how you reacted).

Time date _____

Critical incident_____

How distressing was the incident (score between 0 and 10 whee 10 is the most distressing) _____

What negative thoughts go with this incident

_____

_____

_____

Describe the incident as much detail as possible below. Please include as much information as possible, (for example, how you felt, what happened, how you reacted).

Time date _____

Critical incident_____

How distressing was the incident (score between 0 and 10 whee 10 is the most distressing) _____

What negative thoughts go with this incident

_____

_____

_____

Describe the incident as much detail as possible below. Please include as much information as possible, (for example, how you felt, what happened, how you reacted).

Time date _____

Critical incident_____

How distressing was the incident (score between 0 and 10 whee 10 is the most distressing) _____

What negative thoughts go with this incident

_____

_____

_____

Describe the incident as much detail as possible below. Please include as much information as possible, (for example, how you felt, what happened, how you reacted).

Time date _____

Critical incident _____

How distressing was the incident (score between 0 and 10 whee 10 is the most distressing) _____

What negative thoughts go with this incident

_____

_____

_____

Describe the incident as much detail as possible below. Please include as much information as possible, (for example, how you felt, what happened, how you reacted).

Time date _____

Critical incident_____

How distressing was the incident (score between 0 and 10 whee 10 is the most distressing) _____

What negative thoughts go with this incident

_____

_____

_____

Describe the incident as much detail as possible below. Please include as much information as possible, (for example, how you felt, what happened, how you reacted).

Time date _____

Critical incident_____

How distressing was the incident (score between 0 and 10 whee 10 is the most distressing) _____

What negative thoughts go with this incident

_____

_____

_____

Describe the incident as much detail as possible below. Please include as much information as possible, (for example, how you felt, what happened, how you reacted).

Time date _____

Critical incident_____

How distressing was the incident (score between 0 and 10 whee 10 is the most distressing) _____

What negative thoughts go with this incident

_____

_____

_____

Describe the incident as much detail as possible below. Please include as much information as possible, (for example, how you felt, what happened, how you reacted).

Time date _____

Critical incident_____

How distressing was the incident (score between 0 and 10 whee 10 is the most distressing) _____

What negative thoughts go with this incident

_____

_____

_____

Describe the incident as much detail as possible below. Please include as much information as possible, (for example, how you felt, what happened, how you reacted).

Time date _____

Critical incident_____

How distressing was the incident (score between 0 and 10 whee 10 is the most distressing) _____

What negative thoughts go with this incident

_____

_____

_____

Describe the incident as much detail as possible below. Please include as much information as possible, (for example, how you felt, what happened, how you reacted).

Time date _____

Critical incident_____

How distressing was the incident (score between 0 and 10 whee 10 is the most distressing) _____

What negative thoughts go with this incident

_____

_____

_____

Describe the incident as much detail as possible below. Please include as much information as possible, (for example, how you felt, what happened, how you reacted).

Time date _____

Critical incident_____

How distressing was the incident (score between 0 and 10 whee 10 is the most distressing) _____

What negative thoughts go with this incident

_____

_____

_____

Describe the incident as much detail as possible below. Please include as much information as possible, (for example, how you felt, what happened, how you reacted).

Time date _____

Critical incident_____

How distressing was the incident (score between 0 and 10 whee 10 is the most distressing) _____

What negative thoughts go with this incident

_____

_____

_____

Describe the incident as much detail as possible below. Please include as much information as possible, (for example, how you felt, what happened, how you reacted).

Time date _____

Critical incident_____

How distressing was the incident (score between 0 and 10 whee 10 is the most distressing) _____

What negative thoughts go with this incident

_____

_____

_____

Describe the incident as much detail as possible below. Please include as much information as possible, (for example, how you felt, what happened, how you reacted).

Time date _____

Critical incident_____

How distressing was the incident (score between 0 and 10 whee 10 is the most distressing) _____

What negative thoughts go with this incident

_____

_____

_____

Describe the incident as much detail as possible below. Please include as much information as possible, (for example, how you felt, what happened, how you reacted).

Time date _____

Critical incident_____

How distressing was the incident (score between 0 and 10 whee 10 is the most distressing) _____

What negative thoughts go with this incident

_____

_____

_____

Describe the incident as much detail as possible below. Please include as much information as possible, (for example, how you felt, what happened, how you reacted).

Dream records

The unconscious mind often attempts to work on or resolve issues we are faced with in our lives through dreams. Dreams often contain a rich source of information that can be highly valuable in therapy or counselling. If you decide to make a record of your dreams it is usually advisable to write your dreams down as soon as possible after waking. This section has sheets you can use to make a permanent record of your dreams.

Date of dream _____

Title of dream _____

What emotions did you experience in your dream, for example, fear, uncertainty, happiness?

_____

Theme of your dream

_____

_____

_____

Describe your dream. Please include as much information as possible, (for example, how you felt, what happened, how you reacted, what people were involved, what symbols were in your dream, the environment your dream occurred in). How might you interpret your dream? Is it a reoccurring dream or is it new?

Date of dream _____

Title of dream _____

What emotions did you experience in your dream, for example, fear, uncertainty, happiness?

_____

Theme of your dream

_____

_____

_____

Describe your dream. Please include as much information as possible, (for example, how you felt, what happened, how you reacted, what people were involved, what symbols were in your dream, the environment your dream occurred in). How might you interpret your dream? Is it a reoccurring dream or is it new?

Date of dream _____

Title of dream _____

What emotions did you experience in your dream, for example, fear, uncertainty, happiness?

_____

Theme of your dream

_____

_____

_____

Describe your dream. Please include as much information as possible, (for example, how you felt, what happened, how you reacted, what people were involved, what symbols were in your dream, the environment your dream occurred in). How might you interpret your dream? Is it a reoccurring dream or is it new?

Date of dream _____

Title of dream _____

What emotions did you experience in your dream, for example, fear, uncertainty, happiness?

_____

Theme of your dream

_____

_____

_____

Describe your dream. Please include as much information as possible, (for example, how you felt, what happened, how you reacted, what people were involved, what symbols were in your dream, the environment your dream occurred in). How might you interpret your dream? Is it a reoccurring dream or is it new?

Date of dream _____

Title of dream _____

What emotions did you experience in your dream, for example, fear, uncertainty, happiness?

_____

Theme of your dream

_____

_____

_____

Describe your dream. Please include as much information as possible, (for example, how you felt, what happened, how you reacted, what people were involved, what symbols were in your dream, the environment your dream occurred in). How might you interpret your dream? Is it a reoccurring dream or is it new?

Date of dream _____

Title of dream _____

What emotions did you experience in your dream, for example, fear, uncertainty, happiness?

_____

Theme of your dream

_____

_____

_____

Describe your dream. Please include as much information as possible, (for example, how you felt, what happened, how you reacted, what people were involved, what symbols were in your dream, the environment your dream occurred in). How might you interpret your dream? Is it a reoccurring dream or is it new?

Date of dream _____

Title of dream _____

What emotions did you experience in your dream, for example, fear, uncertainty, happiness?

_____

Theme of your dream

_____

_____

_____

Describe your dream. Please include as much information as possible, (for example, how you felt, what happened, how you reacted, what people were involved, what symbols were in your dream, the environment your dream occurred in). How might you interpret your dream? Is it a reoccurring dream or is it new?

Date of dream _____

Title of dream _____

What emotions did you experience in your dream, for example, fear, uncertainty, happiness?

_____

Theme of your dream

_____

_____

_____

Describe your dream. Please include as much information as possible, (for example, how you felt, what happened, how you reacted, what people were involved, what symbols were in your dream, the environment your dream occurred in). How might you interpret your dream? Is it a reoccurring dream or is it new?

Date of dream _____

Title of dream _____

What emotions did you experience in your dream, for example, fear, uncertainty, happiness?

_____

Theme of your dream

_____

_____

_____

Describe your dream. Please include as much information as possible, (for example, how you felt, what happened, how you reacted, what people were involved, what symbols were in your dream, the environment your dream occurred in). How might you interpret your dream? Is it a reoccurring dream or is it new?

Date of dream _____

Title of dream _____

What emotions did you experience in your dream, for example, fear, uncertainty, happiness?

_____

Theme of your dream

_____

_____

_____

Describe your dream. Please include as much information as possible, (for example, how you felt, what happened, how you reacted, what people were involved, what symbols were in your dream, the environment your dream occurred in). How might you interpret your dream? Is it a reoccurring dream or is it new?

Date of dream _____

Title of dream _____

What emotions did you experience in your dream, for example, fear, uncertainty, happiness?

_____

Theme of your dream

_____

_____

_____

Describe your dream. Please include as much information as possible, (for example, how you felt, what happened, how you reacted, what people were involved, what symbols were in your dream, the environment your dream occurred in). How might you interpret your dream? Is it a reoccurring dream or is it new?

Date of dream _____

Title of dream _____

What emotions did you experience in your dream, for example, fear, uncertainty, happiness?

_____

Theme of your dream

_____

_____

_____

Describe your dream. Please include as much information as possible, (for example, how you felt, what happened, how you reacted, what people were involved, what symbols were in your dream, the environment your dream occurred in). How might you interpret your dream? Is it a reoccurring dream or is it new?

Date of dream _____

Title of dream _____

What emotions did you experience in your dream, for example, fear, uncertainty, happiness?

_____

Theme of your dream

_____

_____

_____

Describe your dream. Please include as much information as possible, (for example, how you felt, what happened, how you reacted, what people were involved, what symbols were in your dream, the environment your dream occurred in). How might you interpret your dream? Is it a reoccurring dream or is it new?

Date of dream _____

Title of dream _____

What emotions did you experience in your dream, for example, fear, uncertainty, happiness?

_____

Theme of your dream

_____

_____

_____

Describe your dream. Please include as much information as possible, (for example, how you felt, what happened, how you reacted, what people were involved, what symbols were in your dream, the environment your dream occurred in). How might you interpret your dream? Is it a reoccurring dream or is it new?

Date of dream _____

Title of dream _____

What emotions did you experience in your dream, for example, fear, uncertainty, happiness?

_____

Theme of your dream

_____

_____

_____

Describe your dream. Please include as much information as possible, (for example, how you felt, what happened, how you reacted, what people were involved, what symbols were in your dream, the environment your dream occurred in). How might you interpret your dream? Is it a reoccurring dream or is it new?

Date of dream _____

Title of dream _____

What emotions did you experience in your dream, for example, fear, uncertainty, happiness?

_____

Theme of your dream

_____

_____

_____

Describe your dream. Please include as much information as possible, (for example, how you felt, what happened, how you reacted, what people were involved, what symbols were in your dream, the environment your dream occurred in). How might you interpret your dream? Is it a reoccurring dream or is it new?

Date of dream _____

Title of dream _____

What emotions did you experience in your dream, for example, fear, uncertainty, happiness?

_____

Theme of your dream

_____

_____

_____

Describe your dream. Please include as much information as possible, (for example, how you felt, what happened, how you reacted, what people were involved, what symbols were in your dream, the environment your dream occurred in). How might you interpret your dream? Is it a reoccurring dream or is it new?

Conclusion

When you have come to the end of your therapy or counselling, hopefully you will have a much greater understanding of yourself. You are highly likely to meet resistance from yourself when you begin to approach change. But when you can get past this resistance, you may learn new things from your new experiences, and you can use what you learn for the future – hopefully, even for the rest of your life. If you notice that you want to resist change, this is completely natural and it happens to us all.

Another area that you may find challenging after you have completed your therapy is habitual behaviour. Much of the time we can find ourselves falling into repetitive loops or habitual behaviours when we become highly emotional. (Habitual behaviours are behaviours that occur automatically.) Many of us use the same habitual behaviours over and over again to deal with our emotions in certain situations, even when we know that our strategies don't work. Hopefully, you can use the contents of your therapy journal to remind yourself of what you have learnt and know that you can now react to things differently.

Notes

Notes

Notes

Notes

Common Medications

Alprazolam: A benzodiazepine prescribed for panic, generalised anxiety, phobias, social anxiety, OCD

Amitriptyline: A tricyclic antidepressant

Atenolol: A beta-blocker prescribed for anxiety

Buspirone: A mild tranquiliser prescribed for generalised anxiety, OCD and panic

Chlordiazepoxide: A benzodiazepine prescribed for generalised anxiety, phobias

Citalopram: A selective serotonin reuptake inhibitor commonly prescribed for mixed anxiety and depression

Clomipramine: A tricyclic antidepressant

Clonazepam: A benzodiazepine prescribed for panic, generalised anxiety, phobias, social anxiety

Desipramine: A tricyclic anti-depressant

Diazepam: A benzodiazepine prescribed for generalised anxiety, panic, phobias

Doxepin: A tricyclic antidepressant

Duloxetine: A serotonin-norepinephrine reuptake inhibitor

Escitalopram Oxalate: A selective serotonin reuptake inhibitor

Fluoxetine: A selective serotonin reuptake inhibitor

Fluvoxamine: A selective serotonin reuptake inhibitor

Gabapentin: An anticonvulsant prescribed for generalised anxiety and social anxiety

Imipramine: A tri-cyclic antidepressant

Lorazepam: A benzodiazepine prescribed for generalised anxiety, panic, phobias

Nortriptyline: A tricyclic antidepressant

Oxazepam: A benzodiazepine prescribed for generalised anxiety, phobias

Paroxetine: A selective serotonin reuptake inhibitor

Phenelzine: A monoamine oxidase inhibitor

Pregabalin: An anticonvulsant prescribed for generalised anxiety disorder

Propanalol: A beta blocker prescribed for anxiety

Sertraline: A selective serotonin reuptake inhibitor

Tranylcypromine: A monoamine oxidase inhibitor

Valproate: An anti-convulsant prescribed for panic

Venlafaxine: A serotonin-norepinephrine reuptake inhibitor

Made in the USA
Monee, IL
26 June 2022

98635352R10077